Translation once meant the removal of holy relics from one place to another. Translation today tries to remove a poem from one language to another, regarding it not as holy, nor a relic, but a human voice praising, crying, telling the shape of another person's life.

For the rest of this agonizing century, translation must be the way of the world. There is no other choice, not merely for understanding, but for survival itself, than for all of us to talk with each other. Since not even jet planes can take everyone everywhere, that talking must be done by translating books, far more than ever before, until half the publications in a year will come from other languages than our own.

The International Writing Program, the only one of its kind, 'translates' writers from all parts of the world to Iowa City, where they write their own books and often translate them or other books from their own country. Associated with this unique Program is a publishing program that envisages a series of comprehensive anthologies of contemporary poetry from the less accessible languages, comprising Korean, Chinese, Japanese, Yugoslav, Hungarian, Russian, Dutch, Indian (Hindi, Urdu, Bengali etc.) and others. In addition, the Program is co-publishing translations of selected works of a number of outstanding individual contemporary poets. In some cases, poets who have been members of the Program have co-operated with young American writers in the translation of their own work or that of others; in other cases, writers who are also expert translators have been invited to Iowa City to work on specific translation projects initiated by themselves or the Program. 'Co-translation' will never replace the traditional method of one person knowing both languages, as in the case of the present volume, but it will greatly expand the resources of translation. At the same time, the test, even with one translator, must always be the quality of the language *into* which the original is translated. A sensitive knowledge of the first language must be matched with a sensitive use of the second language, so that what was a poem in the original becomes again a live poem in the words of the translator(s).

The University of Iowa, the Northwest Area Foundation and the Department of State have supported the Program and its translation efforts w⁻ʰ ᵐᵖᵃᵗʰʸ ᵃⁿᵈ with funds, a beautiful combination.

International Writ...
University ...
Paul Engle, Director   Director

UNESCO COLLECTION OF
REPRESENTATIVE WORKS
EUROPEAN SERIES

This volume has been accepted in the series of translations
of representative works jointly sponsored
by the United Nations Educational, Scientific and Cultural
Organization (UNESCO)
and the Hungarian National Commission for UNESCO

Thomas Mann and Attila József

ATTILA JÓZSEF

Selected Poems and Texts

translated from the Hungarian by
John Bátki

edited by

**George Gömöri
and James Atlas**

International Writing Program

Carcanet Press

First published in the
United States 1976
by the International Writing Program
School of Letters
The University of Iowa
Iowa City
Iowa 52242

ISBN 0 87745 073 0

Printed in Great Britain
by W & J Mackay Limited, Chatham

CONTENTS

6

TRANSLATION is a bridge, not a betrayal. It connects two separate and often distant places, so that people can cross over or linger and enjoy the view. The River Merchant's Wife in Ezra Pound's version of 'Rihaku' is twin sister to her original in Li Po, even though scholars may find fault with Pound's interpretation of words, phrases, and lines.

In making these translations I was fortunate in knowing the language of the originals. I owe thanks to Imre Szász and George Gömöri, of Budapest and Cambridge respectively, for their careful efforts to ensure the lexical accuracy of my interpretations. On the other side, my debts are more numerous: many friends have helped to bring József into this language. I thank Donald Justice for his encouragement to begin the work and for his generous and painstaking help, especially with the earlier poems. Thanks go to Robert Bly for his vigorous and enthusiastic criticism, even if it was not always fully heeded . . . and to David Young for his fine comments on several poems, notably 'Winter Night'.

As a recipient of fellowships from Syracuse University, the University of Iowa, and the Institute for Cultural Relations (Budapest), I thank the individuals at these institutions who made the awards possible.

John Bátki

CURRICULUM VITAE (1937)

I WAS born in Budapest in 1905 and am Greek orthodox by religion. My father, the late Áron József,[1] left the country when I was three years old, and I was sent to live with foster-parents at Öcsöd through the agency of the League for Protection of Children. I lived there until I was seven, and I even started working as a swineherd, like most poor children in the village. When I was seven years old, my mother, the late Borbála Pőcze, brought me back to Budapest, and enrolled me in the second grade of elementary school. My mother supported us—me and my two sisters— by doing washing and housework. She worked at different houses and was away all day, so that without parental supervision I skipped school and played in the streets. In the third-grade reader, however, I found some interesting stories about King Attila and so I threw myself into reading. These stories about the King of the Huns interested me not only because my name was Attila but also because my foster-parents at Öcsöd used to call me Steve. After consulting the neighbours, they came to the conclusion, in front of me, that there was no such name as Attila. This astounded me; I felt my very existence was being called in question. I believe the discovery of the tales about Attila had a decisive influence on all my ambitions from then on; in the last analysis it was perhaps this that led me to literature. This was the experience that turned me into a person who thinks, one who listens to the opinions of others, but examines them critically in his own mind; someone who resigns himself to being called Steve until it is proved that his name is Attila, as he himself had thought all along.

The World War broke out when I was nine, and our lot became progressively worse. I did my share of standing in foodlines: there were times when I stepped into the line in front of a food store at nine in the evening, only to be told, when my turn came up at eight in the morning, that the cooking lard was all gone. I helped my mother as well as I could. I sold drinking water at the Világ Cinema. I stole firewood and coal from the Ferencváros freight station so that we should have fuel. I made coloured paper whirligigs which I peddled to children who were better off. I carried baskets and packages in the Market Hall, and so on. In the summer of 1918 I was taken for a holiday to Abbazia by the King Károly Children's Fund. My mother by this time was seriously ill with a tumor of the uterus, and I had to apply on my own for assistance from the League for Protection of

[1] Unknown to the poet, his father was still alive when this was written. Contrary to family tradition, he did not emigrate to America, but went only as far as Rumania, where he settled and died a few weeks before his son, in November 1937.

Children. For a short time I was sent to Monor. Returning to Budapest, I sold newspapers and trafficked in postage stamps and, later, in the blue and white inflation banknotes. During the Rumanian occupation I worked as a bread boy at the Café Emke. Meanwhile, having finished the five grades of elementary school, I was attending secondary school.

My mother died in 1919 at Christmas time. The Orphans' Board appointed my brother-in-law, Dr. Ödön Makai, now deceased, to be my guardian. Throughout one spring and summer I served on the tugs Vihar, Török, and Tatár of the Atlantica Ocean Shipping Co. At this time I took the exams of the fourth grade of secondary school, as a private student. Then my guardian and Dr. Sándor Giesswein sent me to train as a novice with the Salesian Order at Nyergesujfalu. I spent only two weeks there, since I am Greek Orthodox and not Roman Catholic. From here I went to the Demke boarding school in Makó, where I soon obtained free tuition. In the summer I tutored at Mezőhegyes to earn my room and board. I finished the sixth year of *gymnasium* with excellent grades, despite the fact that, due to adolescent problems, I had several times tried to commit suicide; then as before I was lacking the guidance of a good friend. My first poems appeared at this time; *Nyugat* published some of my poems written at the age of seventeen. They took me for an infant prodigy; actually I was just an orphan.

After the sixth year of *gymnasium* I left school because I was lonely and had nothing to do; I did no studying, for I knew the lessons after hearing the teacher's explanations in class—my good grades testified to that. I went to Kiszombor as a crop-watchman and field-hand, then I did some tutoring. Finally, at the urging of two of my kind teachers, I decided to take the exam for my graduation certificate. I took the exams for the last two years' material and thus graduated a year ahead of my classmates. I had only three months to prepare, however, which is the reason why I got a 'good' in the seventh, and only a 'satisfactory' in the eighth year exam. My grades for the final exam were better: here I got a 'satisfactory' only in Hungarian and in history. It was about this time that I was prosecuted for blasphemy in one of my poems. I was acquitted by the High Court.

After that I was a book salesman in Budapest for some time; then, at the time of the inflation, I worked in an office at the Mauthner private bank. After the introduction of the Hintz system I was transferred to the accounting department, and shortly after this, much to the annoyance of my senior colleagues, I was entrusted with supervising the currency values on accounts days. My enthusiasm was somewhat dampened by the fact that, in addition to my own work, I was often stuck with duties that belonged to my senior colleagues. Nor did they fail to chaff me about my poems, which were then appearing in periodicals. 'I too used to write poetry at your age,' they kept saying. Later the bank failed.

I decided once and for all that I would be a writer and that I would find some employment closely connected with literature. I enrolled for Hungarian and French literature and Philosophy in the Faculty of Arts at Szeged University. I took 52 hours of lectures and seminars a week, 20 hours of which were for my end-of-semester examinations, which I passed with distinction. I could now eat regularly and I paid my rent out of royalties on my poems. It made me very proud that Professor Lajos Dézsi declared me to be competent to undertake independent research. However, all my hopes were destroyed when Professor Antal Horger, who was my examiner in Hungarian philology, called me in and before two witnesses—I still remember their names, they are teachers now —stated that as long as he was there, I would never become a secondary school teacher because, as he said, 'The kind of person who writes this sort of poem'—and here he held up a copy of the periodical *Szeged*—'is not to be trusted with the education of the future generation.' People often talk about the irony of fate: this poem of mine, 'With a Pure Heart', became quite famous: seven articles have been written about it; Lajos Hatvany more than once described it as the document of the post-war generation for 'future ages'; Ignotus, writing about it in *Nyugat*, said that he had 'cradled and fondled this beautiful poem in his soul, he murmured it and hummed it,' and in his *Ars Poetica* he made this poem the model exhibit of modern poetry.

The next year, at the age of twenty, I went to Vienna and enrolled at the University there. I made my living by selling newspapers outside the Rathaus Keller restaurant and cleaning the premises of the Collegium Hungaricum. The director, Antal Lábán, put an end to this when he heard about me: he gave me meals at the Collegium and found pupils for me. I tutored the two sons of Zoltán Hajdu, Managing Director of the Anglo-Austrian Bank. From the frightful slum in Vienna where for four months I didn't even have any sheets, I went straight to Hatvan as the guest of the Hatvany family at their mansion. Then the lady of the house, Mrs Albert Hirsch, paid my travelling expenses to Paris at the end of the summer. There I enrolled at the Sorbonne. I spent the following summer at the sea-side in a fishing village in the south of France.

After that I returned to Budapest. I attended two semesters at the University. I didn't take my teacher's diploma since, in view of Antal Horger's threat, I thought I wouldn't get a position anyway. Then when the Foreign Trade Institute was founded I was employed there for French correspondence. (I think that my former manager, Mr Sándor Kóródi, would be quite willing to supply a reference.) Then I was overtaken by a succession of such unexpected blows that, however toughened I was by life, I simply could not go on. The National Health Service first sent me to a sanatorium, then I was recommended for National Assistance, because of severe depression. I left my job, since I realized I could not stay on as a burden in a young institution. Since then I have been living on my writing. I am the editor of *Szép Szó*, a literary and critical periodical. Apart from my mother tongue, Hungarian, I read and write French and German, I am experienced in Hungarian and French business correspondence, and I am a good typist. I have studied shorthand and with a month's experience would regain my speed. I am familiar with the technicalities of printing and can express myself clearly and precisely. I consider myself honest and I am, I think, intelligent and a hard worker.

OUR century has not been kind to its poets, especially those who happened to live on the 'main thoroughfares' of Europe or were caught up in the maelstrom of revolution and civil war. One did not have to live in Russia or in Spain, though, to become a victim. It could happen in a relatively peaceful and quiet country like Hungary after the First World War, if the poet was unfortunate enough not only to contemplate the major tensions and contradictions of his epoch but to experience them directly. Social injustice coupled with a sense of personal crisis could crush anyone; only an artist could fight back, effectively parrying the blows of 'destiny' with the weapon of his creative will. In the case of Attila József, the poet died a tragic death, but the result of his struggle—a poetry of unusual intensity and authenticity—survived him.

Attila nowadays is a common enough Hungarian Christian name, though it may strike foreigners as strange; while József, the Hungarian version of Joseph, is one of the most common names in many Catholic countries. In this instance, however, József is a surname. This combination of the two names, one historical and unique, the other ordinary and no more than average, sounds particularly unusual, in that Attila József was born in 1905 into a proletarian family. As the poet's sister relates in her memoirs, Attila's father had a dream in which a majestic-looking old man appeared, bidding him to call his yet unborn son Attila, like the King of the Huns, for 'he will become a famous man'. The poet himself writes in his 'Curriculum Vitae' that it was on account of his Christian name, which was unacceptable to his uneducated foster-parents in the village of Öcsöd, that his first important conflict with the world took shape, and, moreover, it was his realization that a king named Attila *had existed* which first led him to literature. Poetry became for him a way to assert his identity; in proving that he was 'not Steve but Attila' he was confirming his right to live.

No doubt this early episode could be interpreted as a sign of latent schizophrenic tendencies; but as a child and a young man Attila József was, though not always healthy or well-fed, and always desperately poor, at least as normal as thousands of other children from working-class families. In fact, the first poem he wrote, while still a child, expressed desires which were fairly characteristic of children at his age and in his social situation:

> Oh how I'd like to be rich
> To eat once roast goose,
> To walk about in a nice suit . . .

His alienation from society was not a simple and inevitable process; there were cycles of forward thrusts, setbacks and realignments, though the intensity with which he experienced his setbacks increased year by year. His poetry (with the exception of some simple and innocent poems written in the early 'twenties) is a truthful record of alienation, both in a collective and individual sense. His social rebellion was a result of his non-participation in society; he was alienated from the existing social order as a consequence both of his proletarian origins and of his frustrated ambition to eke out a living, however modest, that would give him some material independence. József's nervous breakdown, which coincided tragically with a marked improvement in his living conditions, was also due to alienation—from other human beings, from the source of love.

The two alienations, different yet overlapping, promoted one another. Attila's father left the family when his son was only three; 'Mama', the small and frail washerwoman whose memory was evoked so often, died when he was only fourteen. Old Hungary, part of the Austro-Hungarian monarchy, collapsed in a Bengal light of revolution and internecine struggles, and the conservative regime of Admiral Horthy that rose on its ruins did not represent the majority of the population. Thus the young poet's anarchistic outburst, 'I have no father and no mother/ I have no country and no god', was more than a subjective statement; it represented the desperate war-cry of his 'superfluous' generation. This poem, 'With a Pure Heart', earned him a reputation among liberal critics and his expulsion from Szeged University. He left for Vienna, and from there went to France, where he met some distinguished left-wing emigrés and studied French zealously. It was in Paris that he recognized the necessity of participating in the world-wide struggle between 'imperialism and bolshevism', taking sides with those who promised a 'totally different' kind of freedom. His commitment to revolutionary action was still somewhat theoretical at this time, becoming actual only after his return to Hungary and an unfortunate love-affair with a 'bourgeois' girl ('I was in love with a rich girl/ but her folks snatched her away from me', he wrote soon afterwards). Love failed him while society, unable or unwilling to use his talents (the date was then 1929), reduced him to an uncertain subsistence on odd jobs, to periodic starvation and misery. It was a logical act of defiance and self-defense to join the then-illegal Communist Party, the only faction which had vowed to abolish concrete injustices through revolutionary practice.

For Attila József it was also an act of faith in the efficacy of social therapy. The warm-hearted and casual anarchist who had been reading, now Bakunin, now the Bible, and had returned from Paris with François Villon's tough ballads and the Surrealists' weird images in his knapsack, now turned to Marx. And not only to Marx—for a short time József's poetry became subordinated to the actual tasks of 'party work', his language was penetrated by words like 'exploitation', 'class struggle', and 'agitators'. The poet in him, however, was more interested in social reality than in political tactics, so that his Marxism found its proper expression in a series of great frescoes and *tableaux*, odes and elegies describing both the gloomy, 'iron' world of factories, empty lots and slums, and the poet's determination to fight for the liberation of the exploited and dejected poor. What is particularly striking in these poems is their relentless sincerity and authenticity. 'Night in the Slums' and 'Elegy' are free from the Romantic posturing of some revolutionary poets of the period, and from the powerful fist-shaking cum sloganizing of poets like Mayakovsky. József's picture of the slums, of factoryland, dark warehouses and heavy freight trains, is realistic and transcends realism at the same time: things come to life, exude a dull sadness, the landscape permeates the poet's soul. Sombre and depressing as these poems are, in reading them we feel that József alone among his contemporaries understood Marx's contention that the proletariat was bound to rise up against exploitation because of its misery, not because it was intrinsically better or nobler than other classes. It is complete alienation that creates the preconditions of liberation. At the same time, József felt at ease in this environment, even loved it at times:

> Only here can you really smile or cry
> Soul, only here can you bear yourself.
> This is your home.

Socialism remained Attila József's hope and distant ideal, in spite of his conflict with the Communist Party—a conflict that touched on political, aesthetic, and psychological issues. He was criticised in the Party press and pilloried in the text of an 'ideological platform' drawn up by Hungarian emigré writers in Moscow. If we discount the thoroughly ill-formed attack from Moscow, the poet's ideological 'sin' consisted in speaking up for a United Front, an alliance with all genuine democratic forces, before this line became official Party policy. József's dispute with the Party over questions of psychology in relation to the revolution can be traced to his interest in Freud and his conviction that the psychoanalytic method could and indeed ought to be applied to the political behaviour of the masses. In this he was definitely ahead of his times; some of his insights prefigure the work of later Freudian Marxists such as Erich Fromm. The Hungarian poet realized that Nazism in Germany could not have arisen without a psychological conditioning and mental deformation of the masses (later on described by Adorno as the 'authoritarian character'), and that without Freud, Marxism could not give a satisfactory answer to the most relevant problems of a Europe threatened by the mock-revolution of highly-organized Fascism.

While he left no theory of psychoanalytic Marxism, from his poems and prose fragments one can detect József's aim: to find the proper mode of social therapy for a sick world and for a revolutionary movement crippled by sectarian prejudices and delusions. The people in charge of the illegal Communist Party did not share his concerns, but took notice of his 'deviations', and in 1933 he was severed from the Party. There is no record of his official expulsion, but his illegal Party contacts were suddenly discontinued. This was the end of a political 'love affair' for Attila, who experienced his exclusion from this small, sectarian, and tightly-knit community as a betrayal. The circle of friends—mostly liberal and left-wing intellectuals—who surrounded and tried to help the increasingly ill and unbalanced poet in the last years of his life could not replace the lost community that had provided him with warmth and an opportunity to prove himself not only as a poet, but also as a political activist. Some critics regard 'Without Hope', with its extreme, existential expression of alienation ('My heart is perched on nothing's branch') as the crucial poem of this period.

There is something paradoxical, almost uncanny, about the poetic greatness of József's last four years. During this period the schizoid tendencies in Attila's character manifested themselves with increasing severity, but between attacks followed by extended bouts of depression he had brilliant flashes and clear intervals of sanity. Like Hölderlin, it was balanced on the edge of the precipice that he wrote his most radiant and heart-rending poems. Though not a religious believer in daily life (witness the poem 'Guilt'), he finally turned to God in dialectically worded, desperate, and childlike prayers, in which God represents the all-understanding father whom he never really had and always missed: 'Oh god, take me as your son/so I won't be a cruel orphan' ('No One Can Lift Me'). In this poem 'struggle', one of the *leitmotifs* in his poetry, is replaced by a plea, and—in the last line—by the idea of a sacrifice.

This is, almost certainly, an allusion to suicide. It had occurred to him many times before—because he felt that he wasn't loved, or not loved enough. Now love appears to have acquired an almost magical quality; it is the last refuge. In 1935 Attila fell in love with his analyst, enacting the emotional transference of the 'mother image' to another woman. Her refusal impelled him to write 'It Hurts a Lot', a tortured masterpiece. His next and last love, Flora, became the pretext for some unexpectedly lucid love poems (though written to a concept of Flora rather than to a real person). At last the moment came when the poet's mechanism of self-therapy broke down and his death-wish asserted itself with a vengeance.

The temptation to yield to non-being must have been present in Attila's mind for a long time. He could never take his own existence for granted and believed that

> the universe is but extra time
> life like a flood sweeps over
> the banks of death
> beyond the depths of hearts and empty spaces.

The metaphor expresses his predicament with frightening accuracy; he *was* living on borrowed time, and it was a miracle that he didn't collapse years before he did.

In his long, tormented struggle against insanity, Attila József—already an accomplished poet when he wrote 'Night in the Slums'—rose above most of his contemporaries. Hitler, Republican Spain's desperate struggle for survival, the political trials in Soviet Russia, even conservative Hungary's lurch to the right—all served to promote the same condition: *a lack of freedom.* Attila József's protest against this totalitarian condition (and its consequences) is especially eloquent in 'A Breath of Air' and other poems in which he denounces divisive, blind nationalism and predatory Fascism in the name of values shared by both Marxists and idealists: human reason and conscience. That 'peace of freedom' which promised to spring almost inevitably from the revolutionary struggle of the masses turned out to be nothing more than a possible event in the future. Nonetheless, József's dream of a harmonious world remained alive. And though his own life ended under the wheels of a freight train in the 'terrible year' of 1937, his tragedy concealed a victory. His sacrifice was understood by succeeding generations, who rediscovered the depth, gravity, and tenderness of his poetry. Many years after his death these words would be repeated, in open or in secret, in countries suffering social and political oppression:

> Come freedom! Give birth to a new order,
> teach me with good words and let me play,
> your beautiful serene son.

The following selection attempts to present Attila József not only as a poet, but also as a man. Once, while undergoing psychoanalytic treatment, he complained that 'People like my poems—but my poems are not *me.*' The prose texts in this book, 'Curriculum Vitae', the letters, and the short sketch 'Suicide?' provide the human background to József's poetry. The earliest letter printed here, and the poems which are presented in a roughly chronological order, give some idea of the development of his

17

political views—from the acceptance of the law of class struggle to the demand for a broad front against Fascism, the postulate of a democratic and humanistic Socialism. The same development is reflected in József's great political poems, of which the present selection includes only a few. While these poems will be missed by the reader who knows Attila József's entire *oeuvre* in the Hungarian original, many of them present a staggering task for the translator. Poems like 'On the Edge of Town' ('*A város peremén*'), which encase complex Marxist ideas in intricately rhymed and structured stanzas, may be gems of contemporary Socialist poetry, but they should only be translated by a poet whose political commitment and technical virtuosity are comparable to those of Attila József. At present no such poet is writing either in England or in the United States. John Bátki, a young American poet, approached József more subjectively, less taken with the political than with the personal poetry. It may be that József's ultimate greatness lies not so much in poems where he appears as the spokesman for a political movement, for radical or genuinely progressive ideas, as in those where he conveys the quality of a landscape or the essence of a human situation—realistically, yet in images and cadences unmistakably his own. The dialectical, innovatory, and exact character of the poetry comes through in Bátki's translations, which read—despite formal differences from the original texts—as poems written in a contemporary idiom. If they bring József's poetry within breathing distance of readers on both sides of the ocean, this collection will have accomplished its purpose.

George Gömöri

Cambridge, 1972

ATTILA JÓZSEF: CHRONOLOGY

1905   Born in Budapest on April 11.

1908   Disappearance of his father.

1910–12   With foster-parents at Öcsöd.

1919   Death of mother.

1920   Student at *gymnasium* in Makó.

1922   His first volume of poems published, *Beggar of Beauty*.

1923   Drops out of school; takes private exams.

1924   Tried for blasphemy in a published poem. Enters University of Szeged.

1925   His second volume of poems, *That's Not Me Shouting*. Expelled from university for his poem, 'With a Pure Heart'. In September, off to Vienna with two suitcases (one of them containing his manuscripts and books), one stick of salami, a loaf of bread, and 30 shillings.

1926   Letter to Lucie from Vienna: 'Anna Lesznai, Béla Balázs, and Georg Lukács (especially Lukács) all consider me a truly great poet, the first proletarian lyricist possessing international (not cosmopolitan!) qualities, a poet who is destined to receive at the earliest opportunity your preferably sizeable remittance.' September: arrives in Paris. 'My new address: Paris (V), 10 Rue de la Huchette. Write "homme de lettres" in large letters, because these poor, culturally backward Frenchmen still respect such idiots.' Attends lectures at the Sorbonne.

1927   His poems written in French are published in French periodicals, notably in *L'Esprit Nouveau*.

1927–28   Two semesters at the University of Budapest. From a National Student Relief Fund application (in answer to the question, 'Your Earnings'): 'I have been a tutor, newspaper vendor, ship's boy, street paver, bookkeeper, bank clerk, book salesman, paper boy, stenographer, typist, guard in a cornfield, poet, translator, critic, delivery boy, busboy, stevedore, construction worker, day labourer. I cannot give an account of my earnings.' Affair with Márta Vágó. Hospitalized for first time.

1929   His third volume of poems, *Fatherless and Motherless*, of which 100 copies were passed by the author directly into the hands of the public.

1930	Becomes a member of the illegal Communist Party. Lives with Judit Szántó, his companion until 1936.
1931	Essay on 'Literature and Socialism'. His fourth volume (poems and Villon-translations) is confiscated and József prosecuted. Begins psychoanalytic treatment. He is attacked as a Fascist in a document drawn up by Hungarian Communist writers living in Moscow.
1932	His fifth volume, *Night in the Slums*.
1933	The Communist Party severs its association with József.
1934	His sixth volume, *Bear Dance*, including new and selected poems.
1935	Hospitalized for the second time with severe depression.
1936	Becomes editor of *Szép Szó*, an independent left-wing literary review.
1937	January: meeting with Thomas Mann. Police interference prevents him from a public reading of his poem welcoming Mann. February: 'Curriculum Vitae'. April 11, on his birthday: 'Thirty-two years ago—more precisely at 9 P.M. on April 11, 1905, according to the penitentiary's records—after a judiciary detention of nine months, I was sentenced to lifelong correction in a workhouse, on counts of sedition, espionage, betrayal of secrets, indecent exposure, penal idleness, constant creation of scandals, and pathological prevarication. My appeal for pardon having been rejected, I was transferred into the world of incorrigible criminals. The authorities concealed the ineffectualness of the investigation by presenting evidence obtained under torture which, I can testify, lasted an eternity. I maintained my innocence in vain; the court accepted the results of the investigation and the forced confession as the basis of the decision.' Summer: in the Szieszta Sanatorium; his condition deteriorates. November 4: his sisters take him to Balatonszárszó. December 3: dies, a suicide, under the wheels of a freight train.

ATTILA JÓZSEF IN ENGLISH

translations from the poems

Kabdebo, Thomas (ed.), *Attila József: Poems*. Twenty poems translated by Thomas Kabdebo, Michael Beevor, Michael Hamburger, John Szekely, Vernon Watkins. London: The Danubia Book Co., 1966.

Morgan, Edwin, in *New Hungarian Quarterly*, Summer, 1968.

Novak, M. P. and Kiralyfalvi, B., in *Hudson Review*, XX, #4, 1967; *Kenyon Review*, #3, 1968.

Sutter, Ruth, in *Chicago Review*, XVIII, #1, 1965.

Zion, Matthew, and Gömöri, George, in *New Writing of East Europe*, ed. by G. Gömöri and Charles Newman. Chicago: Quadrangle Books, 1968.

criticism

András, László, and Sutter, Ruth, 'Translating Attila József's Poetry', *New Hungarian Quarterly*, VII, #24, 1966.

Klaniczay, Szauder, and Szabolcsi, *History of Hungarian Literature*. Budapest: Corvina, 1964.

Lotz, John, *The Structure of the Sonetti a Corona of Attila József*. Stockholm: Almquist and Wiksell, 1965.

Reményi, Joseph, *Hungarian Writers and Literature*, ed. by August J. Molnar, New Brunswick, New Jersey: Rutgers University Press, 1964.

Sándor, András, 'Attila József', in *New Writing of East Europe*.

THREE LETTERS

to his older sister, Lucie[1]

Paris, VI
25. avril/1927/

My lucie,

have received the hundred *pengős* and the packet you sent. I couldn't write because I didn't have time, i.e. I was too busy trying to figure out what the hell to do with the clothes you sent; I already had two blue and two grey suits, thanks to you, and now how am I going to travel home with all this luggage? At least you could have sent the dresser, too, where I could store them neatly until the sublime moment when I grow into them. Not to speak of the shoes, the quantity of which necessitates two stands in my modest room, lacking which the careful observer may discover shoes both on top of the wardrobe and under the bed. In spite of all this, I found the noble style of the salami terzina and the bacon sonnet absolutely ravishing.

About *Láthatár*.[2] It is well-meaning, yes, but very muddled. How can they publish an article like Zoltán Szász'?[3] And I can't fathom what they would want with their freedom. The day of 'civil liberties' is long past, gone at the time when capitalism grew to reach the stage of imperialism, and the dominant manifestation of economic life, instead of the free competition of shopkeepers—through the accumulation of capital—became the dictatorship of banks and great industrial trusts. With this—as we can experience it on our own skins—goes the militarization of both state and public life, and if we take into account that today, with the division of global territory and the colonization of small states by the great powers, we are living in the age of world wars, it becomes obvious that we can't even speak of 'freedom'.

Today the world's front for politicians means the front of England and Russia, a great mistake, for the real front is that of imperialism and bolshevism, of which the above states mark merely one advanced position. And this front is continually growing and the longer the conflict is prolonged the greater the force of bolshevism, for the strengthening of imperialism

---

[1] József arrived in Paris during the autumn of 1926 and remained there, studying French at the Sorbonne, until the early summer of 1927. This trip had been made possible by the financial assistance of Mrs Albert Hirsch, Lajos Hatvany's sister (see 'Curriculum Vitae').

[2] A short-lived political-cultural review.

[3] Zoltán Szász (1877-1904) was a Liberal journalist and writer, the author of some sharply anti-Communist articles.

also strengthens its contradictions: first, the conflicts within individual imperialist states—between the ruling classes and the proletariat—then the conflicts among the imperialist states themselves, and finally, the contradictions between imperialism and its colonies. The colonies first of all play the role of the source of raw materials, and for the greatest possible exploitation capitalism provides them with capital, industrializes them, thereby creating a local bourgeoisie and proletariat, which bourgeoisie by its very nature strives towards independence, and reacts to the imperialism oppressing it with the highest form of struggle, that is, with war or revolution, and as such, becomes reinforcement to bolshevism in the fight against imperialism.

Compared to today's imperialist capitalism, democratic capitalism, or, more palatably put for the middle classes, bourgeois democracy, means a regression. For the intellectuals there is no way out ahead other than joining one or the other of the two fronts, for the simple reason that no matter how much 'independent good will' there is, one cannot plough in the machine-gun fire between two trenches, whereas this work can be done behind each of the fronts. That imperialism leads to no freedom whatever, does not have to be proved. And bolshevism promises a freedom totally different from what we have known until now. But anyway mankind is so sick that if this would merely bring about, through planned production and division of labour, the physical, bodily improvement of mankind in a few generations, even then it would be worth it if, instead of moaning after a freedom made into an impossible abstraction by imperialism, we would actively participate in the struggle against the real deprivers of freedom. Every moment makes it clearer that one has to join either this side or that, for the fight even for freedom, and especially for freedom, can be fought only through organization, because if the organs oppressing freedom did not exist, then freedom in fact would exist. Even old Moses said, 'Fight law with law'; against organization, and if we want to win, even against disorganization, we must fight in an organized manner. This, naturally, demands selflessness and sacrifices from the gentlemen crying out for freedom; if they are imbecilic enough not to realize the necessity of sacrifice, history will wipe them out without a trace.

Alas, I won't be able to enter the essay contest 'Why Youth Turned Its Back on Freedom'. By the time I got your letter the deadline was over. I doubt if they would publish my articles; I'll write about this, with the accompaniment of a few poems, to the editor . . .

Kisses,
Attila

to Márta Vágó, 1928[1]

Mártus,

this morning I sent a telegram for you in London. To save money, I had to be crafty. What is love? Much love, but this is two words, costing twice as much. So I employed the following brilliant (and natural) ruse, I wrote, Taimbienfort. Seeing this, the baffled girl asked me, 'Was ist das?'—This? A word.—In what language?—Dutch. (This is why I placed the fort after the bien, whereas the other way would have been more correct.)—Dutch?—Dutch.—It's not a contraction of several words? —Oh no.—I am asking because I am responsible for it.—So I began to bargain with her.—My dear Miss, who would find out how many parts this Dutch word is made of! She:—But are you sure it's Dutch?—So I confessed it was French. But not a contraction.—Then please excuse me for a moment, because I am responsible, and have to ask the supervisor if it is really not two words.—Miss, Miss, I am telling you quite sincerely it is not two words.—But are you quite sure? Because I am new here and don't want to break the rules.—Yes, I am quite sure because that's four words, not two. But it means only two words, much love.—What, how many words?—Four.—Four?—Four.—Yes, Miss, I think it would be better if I wrote it in Hungarian.—So I took a new form and made one word of South Kensington and Manson Place. I said, Dear Miss, I am in love but have no money, I must save a *pengő* for otherwise there won't be enough. And I must send the telegram because I promised that by the time my beauty arrives in London, she'll have a letter from me. Since I couldn't write one, I must use the telegraph, for my beauty is a termagant, and will scold me if I don't keep my promise. Then I'll be melancholy and Miss won't be happy either.—She laughed.—You are really nice but I can't help soothe your amorous troubles.—Oh you have misunderstood, I am not trying to save with my heart but with my wits, but if it isn't possible . . . At least send it right away.—Dear sir, it will be there in the afternoon, the afternoon of the twentieth.—Thank you very very much, you are really attentive and kind, and I am happy, if that is possible.—Good-bye.—You should have seen her, she was nearly in tears over the severity of fate— she did not know that after all I did save a *pengő*, and was able to send the telegram. You see what terrible complications are caused when one does not simply love, but loves very much.

[1] Márta Vágó was the daughter of József Vágó, the left-wing economist. She was engaged to marry Attila, who wrote several letters to her in 1928 while she was attending a course on the social sciences in London. The engagement broke up soon after; according to some sources this led to the poet's first breakdown and hospitalization.

I just remembered I owe you a poem, or rather two, since one is due with this letter too. But if I write one now, I can't guarantee the outcome; I am still confused and tired by the already mentioned things[1] (here the letters become tiny, one millimetre tall)—I can tell, because *dans la première partie de ma présente* I have omitted whole halves of sentences. But if I must keep my promise, and I have called you beautiful, and a termagant, I'll give it a try.

> With that blue tie on your neck—
> Whatcha binding, bookbinder?
> —I keep binding, binding, binding,
> books and Bibles and Bakunin.
> Oh your hands are all so calloused—
> and what does Bakunin tell you?
> ⌐—Callouses grow on my hands,
> ⌎ diamonds grow in my heart.

to Mihály Babits

Dear Sir:

My circumstances force me to request you, a trustee of the Baumgarten Literary Foundation, to assist me with the financial resources of the Foundation. The reasons for my request—without any remnant of poetic modesty—can be described as follows.

My wife and I have been, for quite some time now, literally starving. A verifiable fact: the Writers' Fund has for months been allocating to me coffee and a roll at the Club Café; as of January 1st, however, this aid has ceased. My wife, in exchange for housework, eats at various relatives'. This has become painfully embarrassing.

My 'income' for the year amounts to 15, that is, fifteen *pengős*. This amount—like the coffee—has been allocated to me by the Writers' Fund.

Nearly all our belongings—including bed-linen—have been pawned. I have to worry about the rent arrears and the loss of this dreary studio apartment where we still live. Since September 8 I have been unable to pay the electric bill. Today I received a bill of P 19.35 for the past four months payable by Monday—it is Saturday today—otherwise the service will be cut off.

We have no heat. I have no shoes. Or rather I do have one pair of patent leather button-shoes, size 43. I wear a 39. The doorknob to our room has been missing for the past half a year.

[1] In a previous letter József gave an account of a serious clash between his sister and his guardian, almost ending in the former's suicide.

What is needed is not a covered-up wound but painted blood—I could say that we chew on dry breadcrumbs. The truth is that last night, without dinner and without cigarettes, I was chewing on dry breadcrumbs that my wife put away some time ago for use in cooking. I must say I did it not because of hunger but for lack of cigarettes. I've gotten used to hunger.

I am used to it. Why have I chosen this moment to reach for this rather bitter cup? For a week I've been in bed with a fever of 102. We have one narrow sofa on which the two of us sleep. Love is not enough to sleep under the same cover with a man feverish and sick. My wife made a bed for herself on the floor, sleeping on a blanket, covering herself with coats. By the time my fever dropped to 99, she was running a temperature of 101. She took the sofa and I took the floor. Now each day whoever happens to feel worse takes the sofa. Whoever runs a higher fever, coughs and sweats more. And so on.

I am sorry I have to ask for money from you, whom I have offended.[1] I am also very sorry for this painted blood.

Respectfully,
Attila József

[1] An allusion to József's aggressive and, on the whole, unfair review of a book of poetry by Babits, published in 1930.

I WAS nine at the time. Mother went to work early and came home late. Father had left the country two years before. We lived the life of the poor in one room with a kitchen—not that I ever felt we were poor. I was glad to go barefoot from spring to fall and felt like a hero when I stole firewood at the railroad station. I felt sore at times when they caught me and gave me a thrashing, but without these perils I would not have felt like a hero. On such occasions I broke into tears, making use of, rather than actually feeling, our real poverty, and so, lying the truth, I softened the hearts of those grownups and then beat it. Other than that I rarely cried, just in the evenings, when I had to wash my feet. I was the man of the house, teaser of my two older sisters, and on Sunday afternoons, mother's beloved hope.

Once, when mother was away at work, I, for some unremembered reason, wasn't out roaming the streets. It could be winter was coming and I had no boots, I don't remember. From the pocketbook of my older sister—she was already engaged—I stole a cigarette, and instead of taking my booty to the toilet—the only place a poor kid can do what he wants—I lit up in the kitchen. This was open mutiny. Jolán is allowed to do it, but I am not? And I'm the one who is always sent down to the store. And I'm the one, not her, who brings firewood from the park. (On the occasion of such mutinies I always found opportunity to bring up the social significance of these actions I committed gladly and voluntarily even in spite of prohibitions.) So there!

I lit up, although I did take the precaution of huddling in a corner of the kitchen. Jolán, however, smelled the smoke, pulled me out from behind the stove and bestowed two enormous slaps on my face, left and right. I, not so much because of the sting of the slaps (which I can't recall) but because of the incredibly deep moral outrage I felt at this violent curbing of my rights, began to sob, howl, stamp, and rage. Jolán could not stand it for long and left. It could be that she had something to do.

The moment she stepped out I quietly sat down in a corner and, helpless as I felt, planned the darkest of revenges. Hi, said my sister Etus, who meanwhile had entered with a girlfriend. Hi, I hissed back. With that, they went into the other room. (I think they were into fortune telling by cards at the time.)

I decided I would drink lye. Huddled in my corner I relished this thought, now and then thrilled by a sob. I was terribly moved when I imagined myself dead and gone, and how they would constantly remember me with tears in their eyes. Only then will they realize who I was, when they'll be looking for me in vain. And Jolán, that pig, can go to the store by herself, if she wants to. Or else they can send Etus. And mother will tear Jolán apart when she finds out tonight why I died. I began to cry. I was definitely crying as if moved by deep commiseration at the death of someone we dearly love and respect. And I began to feel sorry for poor mother —what is she going to do when it is all over? But she deserves it, I thought, it's all because of her. She is the cause of it. She is the one giving orders around here, she'll be the one to blame for the death of this good, sweet, pleasant, courageous, talented little boy.

I stood up sobered. I went to the cupboard where the lye was kept in a thick brown jug. There was nothing in it though, only a little moisture shining at the bottom. I stood there, dark and motionless. Suddenly I heard mother's words: 'Get five *fillérs*' worth of lye, eight *fillérs* of starch, four *fillérs* of blueing.' Lye, starch, blueing—these things went together, it seems. After some searching I found the starch, quite a chunk of it. I put water in the mug, dissolved the starch, and drank it all. (I still don't know why I didn't drink the blueing.) Then—if you die, you have to collapse— cleverly dropping the jug on the kitchen chair, I collapsed. Stretched out on the kitchen floor, I was waiting for death.

I sighed; I was very scared. I took great gulps and my mouth began to foam. Scared as I was, I still had the effects in mind, and realized that I could afford a truly stunning spectacle only if thick foam was gushing from my mouth. I concentrated on shoving as much of the foam forward with my tongue as I could. But I was trembling all over, and still remember my convulsive movements—I was convinced this was the end.

A great melancholy came over me, and perhaps I would have regretted my deed had it not been for my growing desperation at no one's noticing my death throes. I was seething with rage, especially at Etus, who was calmly entertaining her friend inside. I emitted a few loud groans. I was convulsively clawing the floor with hands and feet. All this affected me as thoroughly as if I really had convulsions, but they were those of my convulsive will. Still no effects. I lay there with my head toward the kitchen entrance, my feet toward the room. I was yearning for someone to enter and discover me. And since I knew that someone could come in and notice me, somehow without getting up I thrashed over to the door of the room until I was near enough to reach it with my feet. Then, somewhat relieved of anger but still sad, I continued my writhing. Etus finally noticed the rattling of the door, because she shouted, Stop it! After this had gone on for a few minutes she lost her patience and came out, saying, still behind the door, Attila are you crazy?!

When she saw me, in the evening dimness, my foaming face, red from crying, sad, tired, and twisted with desperation, she cried out, horrified. Her terror made me even more scared and I began to cry, words falling from me in broken pieces, Dear Etus, I'm dying, I drank lye. (I forgot it was starch that I had gulped down.)

Etus ran down to get the concierge's wife, who put me to bed, and the room was soon filled with lamenting old women. I was terribly afraid and proud. It didn't even matter that after a while the old women forgot about me and began to lament the high price of potatoes.

Etus ran for mother, who left work and rushed home. Shoving people aside, she ran to my bedside. Her mouth was trembling, her eyes full of tears. Then she picked me up, the nine-year-old brat, held me in her arms, began to caress me, and carried me to the kitchen. Softly, almost whispering, she asked me, 'Tell me, son, what did you drink?'

I was almost infinitely happy that mother had taken me in her arms. I forgot all my charges and clung to her. I began to sob again because I felt that I would be completely happy only when mother would take me, caress me, speak softly to me even if I had not done what I had done. Then I pointed at the starch, saying only, This.

Mother sighed, relieved. At this, even I was relieved of my inner load. I forgot about everything and felt only her as she carried me into the room, put me to bed, and covered me. She sat there awhile, spoke a little, softly, only one or two words, I can't recall what, but it was very beautiful.

Then she went out to the kitchen, sent Etus to the store for camomile tea, made a fire, put on a pot of water—I can hear it clink on the stove—and I fell asleep.

THE POEMS OF ATTILA JÓZSEF

Glassmakers

Glassmakers light huge fires
and stir their blood and sweat
into the materials
that boil transparent
in their crucibles.
Then, with what's left of their strength,
they pour the glass into plates
and roll it perfectly smooth.

And when the sun comes up
they carry light to the cities
and to the smallest village huts.

Sometimes they are called labourers,
at other times, poets—
though one is as good as the other.
Slowly they run out of blood
and grow transparent:
large crystal windows to the future
built on you.

Diamond

There is always a time for psalms.

We stand on a diamond mountain,
but our pockets are filled with pebbles.
We have long forgotten the angels we were,
and stuffed our white wings into fat cushions.
Prayers thirst for our strength now
and the stones wear thin under our knees.
The star in our hearts is frozen.

Truly, truly.
The marines have all gone to the bottom.
Now peaceful boatmen sail toward God.

Even the very old men
sit down on benches that stand before things
and preach patience
to the faraway fish of transience.

Truly, truly.
Do not believe then, my friends,
that instead of balls we used to throw our fists!
We must caress everything,
even the hyenas and frogs.

We stand on a diamond mountain.
Severe snow, cover our sins,
loosen our tongues, heavenly light!

O you infinite crystal!

Heavy peasants are straggling home
from the fields without a word.
The river and I are lying side by side.
Fresh grasses sleep under my heart.

A deep calm is rolling in the river.
My heavy cares are now as light as dew.
The man lying here is ageless, without
enemies or brothers—just a tired man.

Evening ladles out the quiet.
I am a warm slice from its loaf of bread.
The sky is resting, and stars come out
to sit on the river and shine on my head.

My eyes, you girls who milk the light,
turn over your pails.
Tongue, you tall handsome whooping young man,
leave your day-labour.
Beast, escape from me to Asia,
to the roots of sweating forests.
Backbone, collapse under the Eiffel Tower.
Nose, you sailing Greenland whaler,
keep your harpoon away from smells.
Hands, make a pilgrimage to Rome.
Legs, kick each other into a ditch.
Ears, surrender
your tympani, your tympani!
Leap over to Australia, my thigh,
you rose-pink marsupial.
Belly, you light balloon, soar
to Saturn, fly away!
Then I shall step out onto my lips,
with a curving shout jump into your ears,
and stopped clocks will start again,
and villages will shine like floodlights,
and the cities will be whitewashed,
and my vertebrae can scatter
in all directions of the globe,
because I'll be standing straight
among the crooked bodies of the dead.

That's not me shouting, it's the earth that roars.
Beware, beware, for Satan is raving.
Lie low on the bottom of clear streams,
flatten yourself into a pane of glass,
hide behind the light of diamonds,
under stones with the small insects,
hide away in the fresh baked bread,
you poor man.
Seep into the ground with cool showers!
Only in others can you wash your face,
it's no use to bathe it in yourself.
Become the edge on a little blade of grass
and you'll be greater than the world's axis.

O machines, birds, leaves, stars!
Our barren mother is praying for a child.
My friend, my dear, beloved friend,
whether it's horrible, whether it's splendid,
that's not me shouting, it's the earth that roars.

A Fine Summer Evening

It is a fine summer evening.

Rumbling trains arrive and depart,
frightened factories are wailing,
soot-black rooftops are blackened by the evening,
newsboys are shouting under the streetlights,
cars are scuttling back and forth,
streetcars are clanging in a great procession,
neon signs scream that you are blind,
walls that trail off into side streets
wave their posters back at you.
Ahead of you, behind you, everywhere,
poster-faced men are scurrying,
and beyond the big city blocks you can see
hallelujah-crying-howling-groaning-swearing
panting-coldly-cunningly-grasping
men
climbing a man-ladder,
and veins are swelling
on the necks of angry avenues.
You can hear the mute office workers' shriek,
the slow footfall of workers going home
as if they were old sages
with nothing left to do on earth.
You can hear the soft movement of pickpockets' wrists,
and from the distance a peasant munching
as he lifts a wide strip of hay
from his neighbour's land.
I who am listening can hear it all.
The worm is whimpering in the beggar's bones,
women are nosing about me,
but I have come from a long way off,
so I just sit on my friendly doorstep
and keep silent.

It is a fine summer evening.

I have no father and no mother,
I have no country and no god.
I have no lover in my bed,
I won't be buried when I'm dead.

For three days now I didn't eat,
not even a piece of bread.
My twenty years are my power—
I'll sell them to the first comer.

If no one needs my twenty years,
the devil takes them, it appears.
With a pure heart, I'll burn and loot.
If I have to, I'll even shoot.

They'll catch me and string me up,
with the good earth cover me up,
and death-bringing grass will start
growing from my beautiful, pure heart.

Sleep quietly now,
on this peaceful evening.
The neighbours are going to bed too.
The street pavers have gone.
Far and clear clanged the stone,
the hammer,
the street,
but all is quiet now.
It's been a long time since I last saw you.

Those busy arms of yours are cool now
like this river with its broad silence
winding soft and slow.
By its banks the trees,
the fish,
the stars
all fall asleep.
I am all alone.

I have done my work. I am tired.
I too shall fall asleep.
Sleep quietly now.
If you are sad
I am sad too.

Silence.
The flowers forgive.

I really love you,
believe me. It is something I inherited
from my mother.
She was a good woman. After all,
she was the one who brought me
into this world.

We may compare life
to a shoe, or a laundromat,
or whatever.
Nonetheless, we love it
for reasons of our own.

Saviours, there are
enough of them to save the world
three times a day and still nobody knows
how to light a match. I'll have to give up
on them.

It would be nice
to buy tickets for a trip to the
self. It must be somewhere inside us.

Every morning I wash
my thoughts
in cold water.
That way they come out fresh as a daisy.

Diamonds can sprout
good warm songs,
if you plant them under your heart.

Some people will stay
pedestrians no matter what they ride,
horse, car, or airplane.

Me, I just lie around
in the morning song of larks
and still make it over the abyss.

                    Let us carefully save our
true souls
like our best suit of clothes
to keep them spotless for the days of
celebration.

Sad

My memories reach up
from under the table.
The breath of the dead
is a breeze and a thought:
who will solve it?

Women and girls huddle together
and shiver inside my beloved.

Somewhere one who is drowning gasps for me:
I bury my head in my palm.

O the music,
the music of the grasses,
have you seen it,
how fine it was.

The warm face of the earth
was caressing me.
I lie down in her eyes
with closed eyes.
I see with her eyes.
The breath of a child
is rocking me.

And then someone
flies out of my heart.
Someone
behaves so badly.

Yesterday afternoon
the earth shed tears.
What shall I do
with my leftover flowers?

Black grass is sprouting on evening clouds,
slowly absorbing their brightness
and sprinkling diamond-air on our sweating faces.
The world is a calm breath
floating over mountains of ice.
Afterwards these melt completely.

If we throw a stone in the air
it doesn't fall back
but turning into a kiss
it flies on great warm wings
up, up to us.
The marrow in our bones
is phosphorescent
like the polestar.
By the light of the two
we can see the bread and water
hiding in the palms of our hands.
I ask the walls
what is the truth,
whereupon they disappear
and I find all of you
sitting around me
under the stars.

The eyelid is made of silky glass:
it caresses us when we close it
but still we go on seeing.
The aloes flower every second in our dreams.
We sleep with our unknown lover,
she is the one who warns us with a light touch
when slowly our blanket begins to slide off.

A transparent lion squats inside black walls.
When I speak to you
I wear freshly ironed clothes in my heart.
I mustn't think of you.
I have my work to do.
You are dancing.
I am starving.
But I am going to live for a long time yet.
For five weeks now I haven't heard from you.
Time raced away on blood-red, wooden legs.
The roads huddle together under the snow.
I do not know if one can love you.
Mute black men play chess
for your words that fell silent a long time ago.

To shove this chair away from here,
to sit down in front of a train,
to climb a mountain with great care,
to shake my bag into the valley,
to feed a bee to my old spider,
to caress an old, old woman,
to sip a delicious bean soup,
to walk on tiptoes in the mud,
to place my hat on railroad tracks,
to stroll around the banks of a lake,
to sit all dressed up on the bottom,
to get a suntan while the waves ring,
to flower with the sunflowers,
or just to give off a deep sigh,
to scare away a single fly,
to wipe the dust from my old book,
to spit a gob into my mirror,
to make peace with my enemies,
to kill them all with a long knife,
to examine their blood gushing,
to watch a young girl as she walks,
to sit idle without stirring,
to set fire to Budapest,
to wait for birds to take my crumbs,
to hurl my stale bread to the ground,
to make my faithful woman cry,
to lift her little sister up high,
if the world wants explanations,
to run away and never be seen—
O you bind me and you free me,
you who write this poem in me,
you bring laughter, you bring weeping,
o my life, you make me choose.

Glasses

A glass is a fresh, clean plant.
It shines in the meadow
and dewdrops land on it.
If a small child looks at glasses,
they ring out softly.

Glasses grow in the heart of springs
but not even glassworkers know this secret.
Young men and girls are always
mistaking each other's glasses.

Once I too took the wrong one.
Since then no glass of water
has been sweet enough for me,
although a bird dying of thirst
discovers many fine glasses beyond the sky.

Finally

I've scrubbed boilers, worked in the fields,
and slept on rotting straw mattresses.
A judged sentenced me, fools mocked me,
and my light shone from deep cellars,
I kissed a girl who, while she sang,
was baking someone else's bread.
I wore hand-me-downs, gave books
to workers, farmers, so they read.
I was in love with a rich girl,
but her folks snatched her away from me.
I ate once every day or two
and came down with ulcers finally.
The world for me was an aching belly,
a churning, slimy, inflamed thing;
our minds, our loves were ulcers burning,
and war nothing but bloody vomit.
A sourish silence filled my mouth,
I kicked my heart so it would shout.
How could I let my free-roaming mind
sing for a wage? Let it cry out!
They offered money to stall my vengeance.
Priests advised me to trust the Lord.
But he who comes home emptyhanded
must bring his axe and carry stones.
My heart is a flashing, winning heart,
I must take sides, and do my part:
I am bound by my stark memories.
But who cares about your memories?
Throw your useless pencil away,
start sharpening the scythe instead!
Menacing, without a sound,
time is ripening in the land.

In China they hanged a mandarin.
Today cocaine has killed again.
The straw is rustling, go to sleep.
Today cocaine has killed again.

Through windows of department stores
the poor see where the money goes.
The straw is rustling, go to sleep.
The poor see where the money goes.

Buy yourself sausage, buy yourself bread,
be careful and don't lose your head.
The straw is rustling, go to sleep.
Be careful and don't lose your head.

A woman who can cook and kiss:
one day you'll find even this.
The straw is rustling, go to sleep.
One day you'll find even this.

O Europe is so many borders,
on every border, murderers.
Don't let me weep for the girl
who'll give birth two years from now.

Don't let me be sad because
I was born a European.
I, a brother of wild bears,
wasting away without my freedom.

I write poems to amuse you.
The sea has risen to the cliffs,
and a table, fully laid,
floats on foam among the clouds.

Coral beads around your neck:
frog heads floating in the lake.
Lamb droppings,
lamb droppings upon the snow.

Golden belt around your waist:
a rose in the moon's halo.
Hempen rope,
hempen rope around my neck.

The motion of your skirt and legs:
clappers swaying inside bells,
two poplars
bending by the river's waters.

The motion of your skirt and legs:
clappers clanging inside bells,
silent leaves
falling into flowing waters.

Since you've been away, things are colder here,
the pail, the milk, the handle of the axe;
split wood falls with a loud thud,
and grows white and numb as soon as it lands.

In a dull field the wind is getting dressed,
its fingers, in a flurry, stop and fumble,
and drop the branches that were pressed
to its bosom: enraged, brittle leaves tumble.

I thought I was in a mild valley,
protected north and south by your breasts,
where dawn flowers in my hair
and evening shines upon my feet . . .

I sit here, thin, and watch you bloom,
world, weed's flower, distant space.
In your blue petals the sky burns out.
A great grey dusk slowly bares its face.

Medallions
(Fragments)

I.

I was an elephant, meek and poor,
I drank the wise waters and the cool,
I stood on a hill and with my trunk
I caressed the sun, the moon,

and raised up to their lips a tree,
a green cricket, a snake, a flint.
Now my soul is human, my heaven is gone,—
I fan myself with horrible ears.

3.

The leech gatherer stumbles, fumbles,
the thin swineherd stares and glares,
over the lake, a hawk floats and hovers,
the fresh cowdung steams and flares.

A tired apple hangs above my head,
a worm has chewed an eye into its heart,
looked through the eye, and saw the bottom:
this poem was a flower, an apple blossom.

4.

Perhaps you are the froth on sugared milk,
or a rustling on a frozen night,
or a knife in leaden water,
or a button that got lost.

The housemaid's tears are falling in the dough,
no kisses here, this place is on fire!
You can still get home if you hurry,
smouldering eyes will light the way.

5.

A pig, but one with jade knuckles,
I sit on a god carved of wood.

Hey velvet mourning, spread out on the milk!
When I am dead, my beard will weigh a ton.

And if I twitch my skin, the sky,
everything rolls down to my belly.
Tiny fat things will swarm all over:
O stars, you little white maggots—

6.

A bright green lizard searches for my fate.
Ears of wheat rattle and pour out their grain.
The pond looks at me when a stone drops in—
and clouds sighed out by mourners,

dawns summoned by wars,
suns that jump and stars that tremble
wander around my peaceful skull.
My temperature is the world's red heat.

8.

The lawyer frozen into amber
wears a tailcoat and peeks out.
He sternly eyes the loving care
lavished by light, breeze, cloud.

As I rot away, the rose blossoms
and cool egrets pick me to pieces.
I shall turn into warm autumn nights
to keep old folk free of goosepimples.

9.

I live in the same bed with my friend
without a wilting lily of my own,
without machine guns, arrows, stones,
and I'd like to kill, like everyone.

While beans are cooking with sibilant pride
you watch me with cabbage green eyes.
My feverish thick lips are trembling.
Again, swallows are feeding me flies.

11.

Twenty-three kings promenading,
with jade crowns upon their heads.
They are nibbling cantaloupes
and new moons shine in their left hands.

Twenty-three kids running around,
with beatup hats upon their heads.
They are gobbling watermelons
and new suns flame in their right hands.

I stand by a puddle and watch it grow,
become a mire, just doing its job.
Tail between legs, a dog
creeps up to sniff my leg.
The heavens are swollen
with their business,
salvation. The bishop's fat lands
blink, and get fatter.
I try to whistle
but only steam comes out
so I steam beautifully
and look important, calm, collected,
like a weed. An old dreamer,
I sink into dreams.

I used to whistle in my breezier days.
Now the rain falls to nourish mud and elders.
Only a cool carrot on the ground,
a harmless paintbrush, and myself
can hear it and give thought.

The sluggish, nationwide rain
laments my thinning hair.

I am a growler, so I growl,
and a stroller, so I stroll:
paddles are never needed on this highway.

My shoes mumble and grumble.
This is too much even for boots.

A pumpkin fidgets. The haystack mopes.
This rain falls on barefoot people,
falls on workers out of work,
falls on the trembling tower,
on estates and on the soft soil,
on cave-dwelling migrant workers,
on cushioned suburban homes,
the rain falls, just doing its job.

Sluggish, nationwide rain,
heavy with complaints.

The raspberry bush squats
and stirs, a greasy scrap
of paper asleep
on its warm arm.

The land is soft, night is a pearl.
Fat, thick-spun foliage.
The mountain's mist
quivers with my song.

I've been working all day
with a drone, like the fields.
How easy heaven is!
My workshop is dark now.

I am tired, simple-minded,
or maybe simply good.
I shiver like the grass
and like the stars.

Pine needles stitch lambskin
shadows to the trees.
The puli moment runs by,
its claws clicking on ice.

The mesmerized folk hem and haw.
Their little houses brood
and pull down greasy hats
of thatch over their windows.

A hen clucks desperately
under the eaves, as if
already an old woman's ghost,
returned to complain.

Indoors, other speckled beasts:
bluish, battered old men squat
grunting aloud from time to time
so they won't sink into thought.

For there is much to think about
when you are too old for the hoe.
Pipesmoke is a fine, soft care,
cotton thread between cracked fingers.

What good is an old man? He drops
the spoon, drools, has to be fed.
And when he tries to feed the pigs
they knock him down and spill the slops.

The farm is soft, the pigsty warm.
Twilight hangs there from a star.
Heaven is hard. A titmouse hobbles
on a twig, and twitters out a cry.

Golden plain, marigold, streaming
and weightless meadow. A small
breeze shakes silver laughter
from a birch. The sky sways.

Here comes a wasp. It sniffs me,
growls, and lands on a wild rose.
The angry rose bows. This summer
is red, but still too slender.

More and more soft stirrings.
Blood-red berries on the sand.
The ripe wheat nods and rustles.
A storm is perched in the treetops.

My summer's end is here so fast!
The wind arrives on tumbleweeds—
and as the heavens crash, comrades,
the blade of a scythe flashes out.

Mother

She held her mug with both hands
one Sunday, and with a quiet smile
she sat a little while
in the growing dusk.

She brought home in a tiny skillet
the food they gave her where she worked.
Going to bed I kept thinking—
the rich always fill their bellies.

My mother was a small woman.
She died early, as washerwomen do:
their legs tremble from carrying,
their heads ache from ironing.

For mountains, they have the dirty laundry.
Their cloudscapes are made of steam.
And if they want a change of climate,
they can climb the attic stairs.

I see her pausing with the iron.
Her frail body, grown thinner and thinner,
was broken by capital.
Think about this, proletarians.

She was stooped from all that laundry.
I didn't realize she was a young woman.
In her dreams she wore a clean apron
and then even the mailman said hello.

Frost

Autumn was wild and brooding.
Now a cool snow would like to fall.
But the season is impatient, drumming
on frost's hard clear window.

This is the time of bankers and generals,
this present time,
this hammer-hardened cold,
this flashing, this knife time.

Steel clanks in the armoured sky.
Frost stabs you, pierces
rags and lungs. O this
screeching grinding-wheel time!

Behind it, how many silent
cold loaves of bread, tin cans,
piles of frozen things!
O shop window time.

And they are screaming, 'Pass me
that rock! Give me that lead pipe!
Kill him! Stomp him! Smash his face!'
O what a time, what a time—

Daylight slowly lifts
its net from our yard
and like a hole in the bottom of a pool
our kitchen fills with darkness.

Silence. A sluggish scrubbing brush
almost begins to crawl.
Above it, a sliver of plaster
ponders whether it should fall.

And night, wrapped up in oily rags,
stops and sighs in the sky,
sits down at the city's outskirts,
then starts to stagger across a square,
lighting the way with a bit of moon.

The factories
stand like ruins,
but inside them
a thicker darkness, the foundation of silence
is prepared.

Through windows of textile plants
moonlight descends
in sheaves.

The moon's soft light is the yarn
fed to the powerful ribbed looms
and until dawn, when work begins again,
machines sullenly weave
factory girls' cascading dreams.

Nearby, graveyard arcades:
steel mills, cement works, powerplants.
So many echoing family crypts.
These factories guard
the secret of a mournful resurrection.
A cat scratches the plank fence

and the superstitious watchman sees
a ghost, flashing signals—
the beetle-backed dynamos
coldly shine.

Trainwhistle.

Dampness rummages in the gloom,
in the leaves of a fallen tree,
and weighs down
the street's dust.

In an alley,
a policeman and a mumbling worker.
Then a comrade, carrying handbills, runs by.
He avoids streetlamps,
sniffs ahead like a dog,
strains his ears, catlike,
for noises from behind.

The mouth of a bar vomits spoiled light.
Its window throws up a puddle.
Inside a lamp swings, choking,
and while the bartender snores and wheezes
a lonely workman stays awake.
He bares his teeth at the wall.
His grief wells up, he is
sobbing.
He drinks to the revolution.

Like molten ore that's cooled,
crashing waters solidify.
The wind, stray dog, wanders around.
Its large tongue hangs out,
touches water, and laps it up.
Silent straw mattresses drift
like rafts on night's tide.

The warehouse is a grounded boat,
the foundry an iron barge.
The die caster dreams a red infant
into metal dies.

Everything is dank and heavy.
Poverty's lands are mapped out
by mildew on the wall.
Out in the barren fields
rags on the ragged grass, and a scrap
of paper. How it wants to move!
It stirs, but has no strength to leave.

O night
your damp and clinging wind
is nothing
but a fluttering of dirty bedsheets.
O night
you hang from the sky like threadbare linen
from a clothesline, like sorrow
dangling from our lives.
O night of the poor, become my fuel,
smoulder here in my heart,
smelt from me the iron,
the unbreakable anvil,
the clanging, flashing hammer,
and the smooth blade of victory
o night.

The night is heavy, the night is sombre.
Brothers, it's time to go to sleep.
Let our souls be free of torment
and our bodies free of vermin.

Water smokes and withered rushes
droop in the flatlands.
The heights are tucked into feathery puffs.
A thick silence crackles
in the snowy fields.

Dusk is fat, greasy, quiet.
The lowlands are flat, neat, and round.
Only a rowboat
clucks to itself
in the pond's freezing mush.

The forest gives birth to shivering times
in its icy branches.
This is where frost snaps
and finds moss for its bony horse
and ties him up.

Vineyards, with a plum tree here and there.
On the vinestocks, soggy straw.
Skinny stakes stand in a row,
waiting for old peasants
to take a walk.

This landscape revolves
around a farmhouse.
Winter's playful claws
crack some more plaster
from its walls.

The pigsty's gate hangs wide open.
It creaks as the wind toys with it.
Perhaps a pig will wander inside
or a cornfield will come running
with its corn!

Small peasants in a small room.
One of them smokes, but only dry leaves.
No prayer is going to help these.

They sit, full of thought,
in the dark.

The vineyard freezes—it's the landlord's.
The trees in the forest crack for him.
The pond is his, too, and under the ice
it's his fat fish that lie waiting
in the mud.

A bumblebee roams by the forest's edge
where a woodpecker pecks and a lizard shines.
Cattle are lowing. The wind is curling
and ruffling the hum of meditative times.

The crumpled yellow land reaches to the
sky's breast. Field of millet, heavy apron,
what is in it? A running brook, and a squat
house, with its little son, the pigsty.

The dusty water does not feel like shining.
Fishscales of a road lie scattered among
rustling trees. On it, the old men of this age,
escaping from their crumbling village.

They hope to find bread under distant yokes.
Their gait is slow, they are brown and bony.
They push small bundles huddled on wheelbarrows.
Above, the soft knapsacks of clouds break open.

Dust hisses and mud spatters at them,
where will they find their work and bread?
A hesitant mosquito wails, and the dry
eyes of the fields stare straight ahead.

If you set out in this world,
better be born seven times.
Once, in a house on fire,
once, in a freezing flood,
once, in a wild madhouse,
once, in a field of ripe wheat,
once, in an empty cloister,
and once among pigs in a sty.
Six babes crying, not enough:
you yourself must be the seventh.

When you must fight to survive,
let your enemy see seven.
One, away from work on Sunday,
one, starting his work on Monday,
one, who teaches without payment,
one, who learned to swim by drowning,
one, who is the seed of a forest,
and one, whom wild forefathers protect,
but all their tricks are not enough:
you yourself must be the seventh.

If you want to find a woman,
let seven men go for her.
One, who gives his heart for words,
one, who takes care of himself,
one, who claims to be a dreamer,
one, who through her skirt can feel her,
one, who knows the hooks and snaps,
one, who steps upon her scarf:
let them buzz like flies around her.
You yourself must be the seventh.

If you write and can afford it,
let seven men write your poem.
One, who builds a marble village,
one, who was born in his sleep,
one, who charts the sky and knows it,
one, whom words call by his name,

one, who perfected his soul,
one, who dissects living rats.
Two are brave and four are wise;
you yourself must be the seventh.

And if all went as was written,
you will die for seven men.
One, who is rocked and suckled,
one, who grabs a hard young breast,
one, who throws down empty dishes,
one, who helps the poor to win,
one, who works till he goes to pieces,
one, who just stares at the moon.
The world will be your tombstone:
you yourself must be the seventh.

SLOWLY, MEDITATIVELY

In the end you reach a sad,
sandy, marshy plain.
You thoughtfully look around,
you nod, and stop to hope.

I would like to look around that way,
with a light heart and no illusions,
while silvery axe strokes
play on the poplar's leaves.

My heart is perched on nothing's branch,
its small body trembles without a sound.
The stars quietly gather
to gaze, and gaze, from all around.

IN AN IRON-COLOURED SKY

Polished, cool dynamos revolve
in an iron-coloured sky.
O noiseless constellations!
Word-sparks fly from my teeth—

Inside me, the past is falling
like a silent stone through space.
This blue and mute time floats away.
A swordblade flashes: it's my hair—

My moustache, fat caterpillar, droops
over my mouth, whose taste is gone.
My heart aches. Words grow cold.
But who is there to speak to—

Be disciplined.

Summer
is gone.
Over lumps of earth like coal
a fine ash shivers in the air.
Silence.
The fragile glass of the atmosphere
scratched by a twig's sharp point:
what a lovely cruelty. A small
silver scrap—maybe a ribbon—
clings fiercely to a bush
for the sake of all the smiles
and all the embraces caught
in the gnarled branches of the world.

Old calloused mountains in the distance!
hands that have grown heavy
that shift from time to time
guarding
the sunset's fire
the steaming farmhouse
the valley's round silence
the breath of mosses.

A farmhand is going home. His heavy
body gazes at the ground.
A cracked hoe bounces on his shoulder,
its shaft and iron bleeding.
He is walking home from life itself,
his body and tools
growing heavier and heavier.

Like smoke
from a chimney throwing sparks
night flies up with its stars.

This blue and iron night comes floating
on bells that slowly toll.

My heart stands still, forever,
and something else—not death,
maybe the land—is throbbing.
Together the winter night,
winter sky and winter metal
make a bell.
Earth is the clapper, this hammered earth,
this swaying weight.
Its voice is my heart.

A memory of clanging. Winter struck
the anvil, repairing with iron
the loose door of the sky's great vault
through which fruit, wheat, hay, and light
poured out all summer.

This winter night shines
like thought.

Silent silver darkness
padlocks a moon over the world.

A raven flies across cold space
and silence freezes. Bone, can you
hear the silence?
Molecule
clinking against molecule.

In what showcase can you see
such glitter as this?
A branch raises its dagger
against the frost.
Waste places send up
a hovering black sigh—
a flock of crows in the fog.

Inside this winter night
is a smaller, separate winter night:
a freight train crossing the plains.
Stars revolve and die out
in its column of smoke
infinite in length and
no wider than an arm.

Trapped on the frozen tops of boxcars,
the light of this winter night
scurries like a mouse.

Winter mists the city.
But speeding toward town on flashing rails,
on blue frost, is the light
of this yellow night.

It sets up its workshop in the city,
to hammer the cold steel blade of pain,
light of this rigid night.

Near the edge of the city
light falls from a streetlight
like wet straw.
On a corner, a clattering
trembling overcoat
—a man—
sits huddled like a pile of dirt,
but it's no use. Winter
still steps on his toes.

Where a rustyleafed tree
leans out from the dark,
like an owner pacing his property
I measure the winter night.

Yellow grass grows on the sand.
This wind is a bony old woman,
this puddle is a nervous beast,
the sea is calm and tells a tale.

I softly hum my inventory.
My home is an overcoat for sale,
a sunset fallen on the dunes.
I cannot go on like this.

Everything shines: time's teeming
coral reef, the lifeless world,
birch tree, woman, tenement—
through the blue currents of the sky.

Elegy

Like a dense downdrift of smoke
between land and leaden sky,
my spirit hangs low,
close to the ground.
It sways, it cannot fly.

O my hard spirit, supple imagination!
Follow reality's heavy tracks,
take a look at yourself here,
where you came from.
Here, under a sky at other times so dilute,
near a solitary, gaunt, bare wall,
poverty's sullen silence
menacing, pleading,
washes away the grief
hardened on a brooding heart
and stirs it
into those of millions.

Man's whole world is made here,
where everything is in ruins.
In an abandoned factory yard
a hardy dandelion opens its umbrella.
The days go down
the faded steps of broken little windows
into dampness, into shadows.
Answer now:
are you from here?
Are you from here, so that you are never left alone
by the grim desire to be
like those other sufferers
into whom this great age wedged itself
to distort and deform their every feature?

Here you can rest, where the crippled
picket fence, with its harsh cries,
upholds and protects
a greedy moral order.
Can you recognize yourself? Here,

waiting for a well-constructed, fine
and concrete future,
are souls with the emptiness of vacant lots
lying around idle, mournful,
dreaming of tall buildings that weave
the noise of life. The tortured grass
is watched by glazed, fixed eyes:
bits of broken glass in the mud.

From time to time a thimbleful of sand
rolls from a mound. And at times
a blue or green or black fly
buzzes by,
drawn here from richer regions
by human waste and rags.
In its own way
the tormented soil
lays the table even here:
yellow grass blooms in a rusty pot.

Can you tell
what consciousness, what barren joy
attracts and drags you
relentlessly to this place?
What rich suffering throws you here?
This is how the child
who was shoved and beaten by strangers
returns to his mother,
Only here can you really smile or cry.
Soul, only here can you bear yourself.
This is your home.

Ode

I sit on a glittering rock.
Young summer's light breeze
floats like the warmth
of a dinner for two.
I am getting my heart used to silence.
It isn't very hard to do—
the past comes swarming back.
My head is bowed, my hand
drops.

I look upon the mountain's mane:
each leaf reflects
the light of your face.
On the road no one, no one,
yet in the wind I see
the flutter of your skirt.
And under fragile branches
your hair tumbles forward,
your breasts quiver softly
and, as the brook runs by,
laughter springs again
from the round white pebbles
of your teeth.

2.

O how I love you
who could bring to words
both solitude which furtively plots
in the deepest hollows of the heart—
and the universe.
Who, like a waterfall from its own thunder,
part from me and run quietly on,
while I, among the summits of my life,
in the nearness of the far, resound
and scream and fling against the earth and sky
my love for you, sweet stepmother.

3.

I love you like a child his mother,
or silent caves their depths.
I love you like rooms love light,
the soul loves flames, and the body, peace.
I love you like the living
love life until they die.

I save each of your gestures, smiles, words
as the earth keeps fallen things.
The acid of my instincts etched you
into my mind's metal,
so that your beautiful, dear form
becomes and fills all meaning.

Minutes march by with a clatter,
but you reside in silence in my ears.
Stars flare up and fall,
but you stand still in my eyes.
The taste of you, like silence in a cavern,
lingers in the coolness of my mouth,
and your delicately veined hand
holding a glass of water
floats before my eyes.

4.

What stuff am I made of
that your glance can cut and shape me?
What soul, what light,
what magic enables me
to roam in this empty fog
through the rolling regions
of your rich body?

And like the word entering the opened mind,
I descend into your mysteries.

Your arteries and veins are rosebushes
quivering ceaselessly.
They circulate the endless stream
so that love may flower upon your face

and your womb may be blessed with fruit.
The sensitive clay of your stomach
is embroidered through and through
by tiny rootlets weaving their fine thread
into nodes, swirling, unravelling,
so that the cells in your fluids can gather
into flocks and the thickets of your leafy lungs
may whisper their own praise.

Timeless matter moves serenely
in the tunnels of your bowels.
Even slag gains a richer life
in your kidneys' fountains.

Inside you, undulating hills arise,
constellations tremble,
lakes shift, factories work,
a million living creatures,
insects,
seaweed,
cruelty, and goodness stir,
the sun shines, and the dim northern light shimmers.
An unknowing eternity
wanders in your body.

5.

These words
drop before you
like clumps of clotted blood.
Life is stuttering,
only a law can speak clearly.

My hard-working organs, that
give me birth from day to day,
are getting ready to be silenced.

But until then, they all cry out,
to you, the only one,
whom they chose from the multitude
of two thousand million,
o you soft cradle, firm grave,
living bed, take me into you!

(How high the sky is at dawn!
Armies glitter in its ores.
This brilliance hurts my eyes.
I think that I am lost.
I can hear my heartbeat
fluttering above me.)

6.

Envoi

(The train is taking me after you,
I may even find you today.
Perhaps my burning face will cool
and perhaps you'll quietly say,

'Take a bath in the warm water.
Here's a towel, get yourself dry.
Dinner's cooking, to soothe your hunger.
This is your bed, where I lie.')

Freight Trains

Freight trains are pulling in.
A slow clanking
lightly handcuffs
the silent landscape.

Like an escaped prisoner
the moon flies free.

Broken stones rest
on their shadows,
sparkling
for themselves.
They are in place
as never before.

From what huge darkness
was this heavy
night chipped?
It falls on us
as a piece of iron falls
on a speck of dust.

Desire,
born of the sun,
when the bed is embraced
by shadow,
could you keep watch
through that whole night as well?

Shears chatter. Sister,
trimming the lawn,
stops. Even from behind
you can see her yawn.

The radio squirms. Wings
buzz on the windowpane,
breezes dance
on the soft grass.

Time pretends to be nothing.
It stops. It's a warm puddle.
Still, it floats away:
a flower shivers.

I can't tell whether
I am asleep or working.
My wife sets the table
with a fine white cloth.

The sky is filled
with a cinematic light.
Wild strawberries shine
in a glass bowl.

I am happy. My love
sews by my side.
We listen to an old
freight train go by.

1.

Dawn has untied the sky from the earth
and at its clear soft word
insects and children, like ripe grain,
roll out into the daylight.
There is no haze in the air,
this sparkling clarity floats everywhere.
Overnight, like small moths,
leaves have covered the trees.

2.

In my dreams I saw paintings
splashed with blue, red, yellow
and I thought this was the order of the world,
not a speck of dust out of place.
Now my dreams seem to be pale shadows
in my limbs, and the iron world is the rule.
During day a moon rises within me
and at night a sun shines inside.

3.

I am thin. At times I eat only bread.
Among the idle chatter of some minds
I search, free and free of charge, for
something more certain than the fall of dice.
True, I didn't eat roast beef too often,
or cuddle a small child near my heart—
but even the trickiest cat can't catch at once
the mouse outside and the one in the house.

4.

Just like a pile of split wood,
the world lies in a heap.
Each thing is pushed and squeezed
and held in place by others
so that everything is determined.
Only what is not can turn into bush,

only what will be can become flower.
The things that exist fall into pieces.

5.

At the freight station I had
flattened myself against a tree
like a piece of silence. Grey weeds
touched my mouth, raw and strangely sweet.
Dead still, I watched the watchman, trying
to outguess him, afraid of his stubborn
shadow on the silent boxcars,
on the shiny, dewy lumps of coal.

6.

You see, the suffering is deep inside,
but the reasons for it lie out there.
The world is your wound. It burns and throbs,
and you feel the fever, your soul.
You are a slave as long as you have to
rebel. You will be free when you stop
building yourself the kind of house
into which landlords like to settle.

7.

I looked up in the night
and saw the cogwheel of the stars.
The loom of the past was weaving laws
from glittering threads of chance.
Then, from my steaming dreams
I looked up at the sky again
and saw that the fabric of the law
would somehow always have its flaw.

8.

Silence listened as the clock struck one.
You could look up your childhood—
even among these damp cinder blocks
it is possible to imagine some freedom—
so I thought. But just as I stood up
the constellations and the stars
lit up like prison bars
above a silent cell.

9.

I have heard iron crying,
I have heard the rain laugh.
I have seen the past shattered, and know
that only ideas can be forgotten.
Now I see all I can do is love
and submit to the weight of my burden.
But why must I forge a weapon
out of you, golden consciousness!

10.

An adult is someone who has
no father and no mother in his heart,
who knows that he receives life
as something extra on death's part,
and, like a found object, can return it
any time—that's why he keeps it.
He is nobody's god or priest,
not even his own.

11.

I have seen happiness face to face:
it was flabby, blond, and weighed four hundred pounds.
Its curly smile wavered
above the harsh grass of the farmyard.
It plopped down into a lukewarm puddle,
blinked and grunted in my direction.
I can still see the hesitant light
fumbling in its fluffy hair.

12.

I live by the railroad tracks.
I watch the trains go by.
The shining windows fly
in the swaying flax darkness.
This is how in eternal darkness
the lit-up days speed by
and I stand in the light of each compartment,
leaning on my elbows, silent.

The little village is a stack of red tiles
steaming slowly like a plate of stew.
The evening is mild and lazy.

Here and there, a slender wisp of smoke
—or hope—wavers on a chimney's edge
(which way to fly?) and waves over the land.

Darkness fondles a slim young locust tree
whose small breasts quiver and send up
a tiny sigh, an air butterfly.

The soft bush of brooding covers me with silence.
A dog's bark falls without a sound
on vast stretches of velvet around me.

Women light the lamps. The twitching,
straining flames want to fly,
like oppressed souls, into the sky.

They flicker out. One light is left
in the field, the motherly moon.
The fat hand of an elder branch reaches out to it.

A chipped, muddy old brick is washed
in streams of eternal happiness.
Frogs in the dewy grass are emerald Buddhas.

Wild oats with drawn swords bend their heads low.
Now the beatup barn becomes
strength and beatitude.

Inside, as if something had just broken
the silence. A clink. A sound for thought, not for
the ear. A sound whose only depth is silence.

And as knowledge dawns here, the words
for understanding are already in the air:
'shovel', 'plough',

words because the farmer says them to the sun,
the rain, the land. I use these words
to trust all this to time's care.

Words that smile on a child
or pat a horse's back. Words
with clear, meaningful syllables.

I listen to the dreaming village.
Troubled dreams fly over us and prod
the shadows of sleeping blades of grass.

Sky, fields, whips, boots, knives are all asleep.
So are the clear wide openings between the boughs
and the spaces in between the leaves.

The farmers are asleep, the raw, slow-spoken
withered farmers. I sit on a small mound, like
sorrow on their hearts. I keep the watch.

Guilt

Oh yes, I am a hardened sinner,
although I feel all right.
Only one thing bothers me:
if I am guilty, where is my crime?

And I am guilty, no doubt.
But no matter where I look
I just can't find my crime.
Maybe it's more basic than I thought.

I search for this crime like a miser
out to find his vanished gold.
I left my mother for its sake
and my heart isn't made of stone.

One day I shall find it
among the champions of righteousness.
Then I'll have to confess.
All my friends will be invited.

I will admit that I have killed.
I don't know the victim: perhaps
it was my father. I just looked on
while he bled away one night.

I stabbed him with a knife. I won't
elaborate. We are human, and some day
each one of us will fall, stabbed.
Now I have confessed.

And so I wait, I must, to see
who will begin to ponder,
who will be too busy to stay,
and who terrified but happy.

Then I'll see that warm
signal in one's eye to tell me
there are others here like me,
I am not the only one . . .

But maybe my crime is too childish,
too simple-minded.
Then the world will have to shrink,
and I'll let it play on.

I don't believe in God. But if
there is one, He shouldn't bother with me.
I shall absolve myself.
And those who are alive will help.

Mother, my fever is ninety-eight point six,
and you are not here to take care of me.
Instead, like an easy woman, when called,
you stretched out by death's side.
I try to piece you together from soft
autumn landscapes and women dear to me,
but I can see there won't be time.
This fire is burning me away.

It was the end of the war
when I went to the country that last time.
In the city, all the stores were empty—
no food, not even bread.
I lay flat on my belly on top of a boxcar
to bring you flour and potatoes in a sack.
I, your stubborn son, brought a chicken for you.
But you weren't there.

You took yourself and your sweet breasts
from me and gave them to maggots.
The words you used to scold, to comfort
were nothing but cheating, lying words.
You cooled my bowl of soup, you stirred it,
'Eat, my baby, grow tall for me.'
Now your empty mouth bites into damp and grease
—o you have deceived me.

I should have devoured you! You gave your own
dinner, but did I ask for it? And why did you
break your back doing all that laundry?
So that the coffin might straighten it out?
I would be glad to have you beat me once more.
I'd be happy, because I could hit you back.
You are worthless! You just want to be dead!
You spoil everything! You are a ghost!

You are a greater cheat than any woman
that ever deceived me. You wailed,
you gave birth out of love,

—and then you stole away.
O you gipsy, you wheedled, you gave
only to steal it back in the last hour.
Your child wants to swear and curse—
mother, can't you hear? Stop me!

Slowly the mind calms down,
the myths run out.
The child who clings to his mother's love
sees how foolish he has been.
Every mother's son is let down in the end,
either deceived, or else trying to cheat.
You can try to fight, and you'll be killed.
Or else make your peace—and die.

Who can forbid my telling what hurt me
   on the way home?
Soft darkness was just settling on the grass,
   a velvet drizzle,
and under my feet the brittle leaves
tossed sleeplessly and moaned
   like beaten children.

Stealthy shrubs were squatting in a circle
   on the city's outskirts.
The autumn wind cautiously stumbled among them.
   The cool moist soil
looked with suspicion at streetlamps;
a wild duck woke clucking in a pond
   as I walked by.

I was thinking, anyone could attack me
   in that lonely place.
Suddenly a man appeared,
   but walked on.
I watched him go. He could have robbed me,
since I wasn't in the mood for self-defence.
   I felt crippled.

They can tap all my telephone calls
   (when, why, to whom.)
They have a file on my dreams and plans
   and on those who read them.
And who knows when they'll find
sufficient reason to dig up the files
   that violate my rights.

In this country, fragile villages
   —where my mother was born—
have fallen from the tree of living rights
   like these leaves
and when a full-grown misery treads on them
a small noise reports their misfortune
   as they're crushed alive.

This is not the order I dreamed of. My soul
   is not at home here
in a world where the insidious
   vegetate easier,
among people who dread to choose
and tell lies with averted eyes
   and feast when someone dies.

This is not how I imagined order.
   Even though
I was beaten as a small child, mostly
   for no reason,
I would have jumped at a single kind word.
I knew my mother and my kin were far,
   these people were strangers.

Now I have grown up. There is more foreign
   matter in my teeth,
more death in my heart. But I still have rights
   until I fall apart
into dust and soul, and now that I've grown up
my skin is not so precious that I should put up
   with the loss of my freedom.

My leader is in my heart. We are
   men, not beasts,
we have minds. While our hearts ripen desires,
   they cannot be kept in files.
Come, freedom! Give birth to a new order,
teach me with good words and let me play,
   your beautiful serene son.

Death is lurking
inside, outside.
Like a scared mouse

you run shaken
to your woman for protection
in her arms, her knees, her lap.

You are lured there
by desire for that soft warmth,
you are thrown there by your need.

That's why all who
find a woman make love to her
till their lips turn white and blue.

They all need love's
double burden, double treasure.
The lover who cannot find love

is as homeless
and as helpless as a wild beast
doing its need in the open.

You will find no
other refuge, even if you
have the strength to knife your mother.

I have someone
who knows my words and their meaning
but she still shoves me away.

Like this, I have
no place in life. My spinning head
whirls fear and pain

like a rattle
in a child's hands,
shaken because he's alone.

What should I do,
fight her? win her?
I won't be ashamed to find out

since I cannot
last much longer. The sun
stuns me, dreams terrorize me.

I drop away
my 'culture' like clothes falling
from lovers before they make love.

Who says that I
must suffer alone while she watches
death slapping me around?

Newborns suffer
when the mother is giving birth.
But the pain is eased by sharing.

And for me, my
painful song brings only money.
Then comes shame and more agony.

Help me! Children,
make your eyes burst
when she walks by.

Babies,
scream out under
boots and tell her: it hurts a lot.

Faithful dogs, get
run over and
howl to her: it hurts a lot.

Pregnant women,
abort your load
and cry to her: it hurts a lot.

Healthy people,
fall and crumble,
mumble to her: it hurts a lot.

Men, who
tear each other for a woman,
don't hold it back: it hurts a lot.

Stallions, bulls,
gelded to pull the master's yoke,
bellow at her: it hurts a lot.

Mute fish,
when you bite the
hook, gape at her: it hurts a lot.

All living things,
everything that shivers in pain,
burn your homes, the green wilderness,

with charred bodies
come to her when she falls asleep
and moan with me: it hurts a lot.

Let her hear it
all her life; she denied her own
worth. For sheer pleasure, she has taken

the last refuge
inside, outside,
from a man who's trying to hide.

My eyes are jumping from my head.
If I go crazy, please don't hurt me.
Just hold me down with your strong hands.

When my whole being begins to squint,
don't show your fists—I won't see—
and don't snatch me back from nothingness.

Think it over: in this world I have nobody,
nothing. What I used to call 'me'
exists no more. I chew on its last pieces

as I write this poem.
Like a reflector in space, a naked glare
searches my insides: What did I do wrong

so that no one answers me,
and the woman who is mine won't love me?
People, do not believe my baffling sins.

Later, the decaying black soil will clear me.

Don't give away your goods
when you're at the end of the line.
Shed your blood for something
that can make you cry.

You can still look on
at the slowly turning sky.
Shape your destiny now, you
who are so slow to cry.

Let your heart wait
for what your eyes already see.
And let your eyes see
what you hide in your heart.

'Son, what have you been up to?'
Your silent mother waits
for you. She is worried.
She ignores your death.

No one can lift me any more,
I am sunk deep into mud.
O god, take me as your son,
so I won't be a cruel orphan.

Gather me up, shape me, form me,
help me to do what they force me,
to praise you and to deny you,
help me in both my needs.

You know my heart is a small child's.
If I deny you, do not deny me,
do not blind the soul in me,
let it look into heaven.

I have grown used to agony
since I took your cares upon me.
Now in the furrows of the shade-world,
let it be you watching over me.

Tell all the people I love
to have a kinder heart toward me.
O hear me out, hear out my case
before I give the final sacrifice.

Only he should read my poems
who loves me and knows me well
and has sailed through nothingness
and like a seer can foretell

the future, because silence in his dreams
has taken on a human shape
and in his heart at times appear
the tiger and the gentle deer.

I saw beauty, sweetness: I was
thinking of a rose.
And reality, like a falling rock,
crashed down on my head.

But even the rock is an image.
It's best to say this simply,
the daily grind has
taught me.

My instincts were on the right track.
When the man entered, they roared
like waves, 'He's here
to disconnect the lights.'

The knife lay on the table.
(I was sharpening a pencil.)
To stab him would have meant
getting even with everything.

I was desperate: all would be
dark and sad around me.
But though animals may defend their lairs,
ours is a different war.

Violence would have been weakness.
I'd lose, and what's worse, lose
my kindness. Law and order
means the rule of money;

warfare has changed its rules.
Our heroes never touch their guns.
They just throw banknotes that
explode into smallchange shrapnel.

Having reasoned this out, I said hello,
turned in and went to sleep.
I awoke to the light
of the full moon and the smiling stars.

I Crawled

I crawled on all fours. My standing God
looked down and refused to raise me.
It was this freedom that made me understand
some day I'll be able to stand on my own.

God helped me by not helping me.
There could be flame but no ashes.
As many truths, so many loves.
He stayed with me by leaving me alone.

My body is weak, may fear protect it!
But I am awaiting my love with a smile
because faith is keeping me company
as the world reels through empty space.

I finally found my home,
the land where my name
is correctly spelled above the grave
where I'm buried—if I'm buried.

This earth will take me in
like an alms box.
No one wants a worthless coin
left over from the days of war,

or the iron ring engraved with
the fine words: new world, rights,
land. Our laws are still for war
and gold rings are preferred.

I was alone for a long time.
Then many came to visit me.
'You live alone' they said, though
gladly I would have lived among them.

That's how I lived, in vain,
I'll be the first to say.
They made me play the fool.
Now even my death is useless.

While I lived, I tried
to stand up against the whirlwind.
The joke is, I harmed less
than I was harmed.

Spring is fine, and so is summer,
but autumn's better, and winter's best
for one who finally leaves his hopes
for a family and a home to others.